All About the U.S. Government

Dona Herweck Rice

Branches of Government

Executive Branch
(enforces laws)

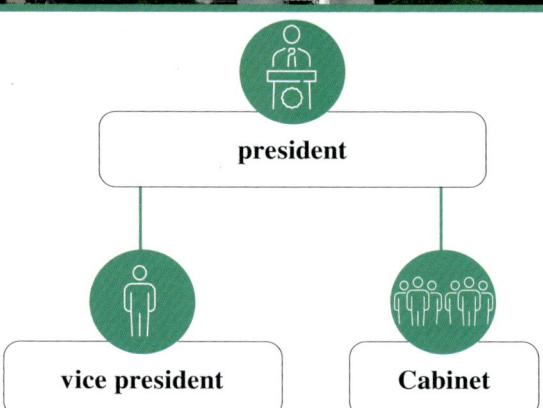

president

vice president

Cabinet

Legislative Branch (makes laws)

House of Representatives

Senate

Judicial Branch (interprets laws)

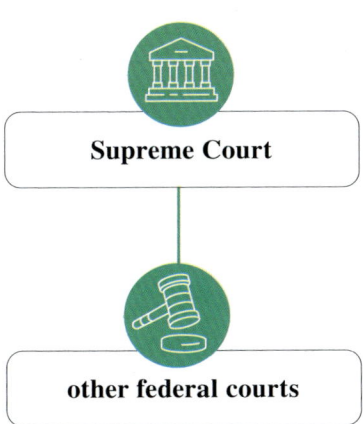

Supreme Court

other federal courts

can declare executive actions unconstitutional

appoints federal judges

**Executive Branch
(enforces laws)**

Judicial Branch
(interprets laws)

- can declare laws unconstitutional

- can impeach judges
- approves judges

- can veto legislation
- can call Congress to session

Legislative Branch
(makes laws)

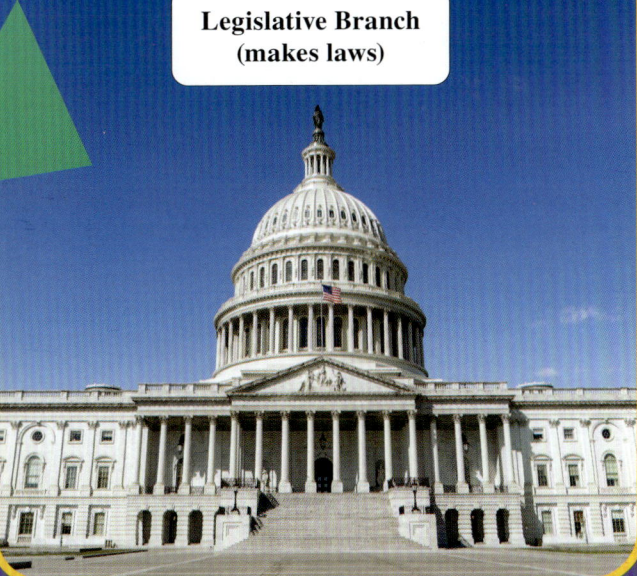

- can override a veto
- can impeach the president

People in the Federal Government

president

vice president

justices

senators

representatives

citizens

governor

mayor

city council

school board

citizens

Federal Government Buildings

White House

United States Capitol

Supreme Court

Treasury Building

Pentagon

state capitol building

IOWA

Des Moines

capital city of a state

city hall

school

park

attend community meetings

volunteer

protest

send a message to representatives

through the press

community cleanup

Participation Through Voting

learning about candidates

canvassing

polling place

voting

born in the
United States

parent is a citizen

naturalization

Declaration of
Independence

Bill of Rights

amendments

U.S. Constitution

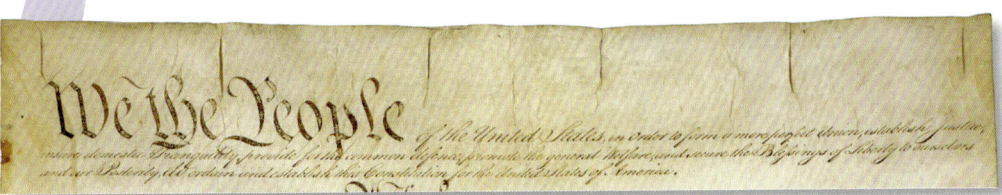

Preamble

Government Symbols

bald eagle

Liberty Bell

Statue of Liberty

Uncle Sam

The U.S. Flag

star

stripe

Nicknames

- Stars and Stripes
- Old Glory
- The Star-Spangled Banner
- The Red, White, and Blue

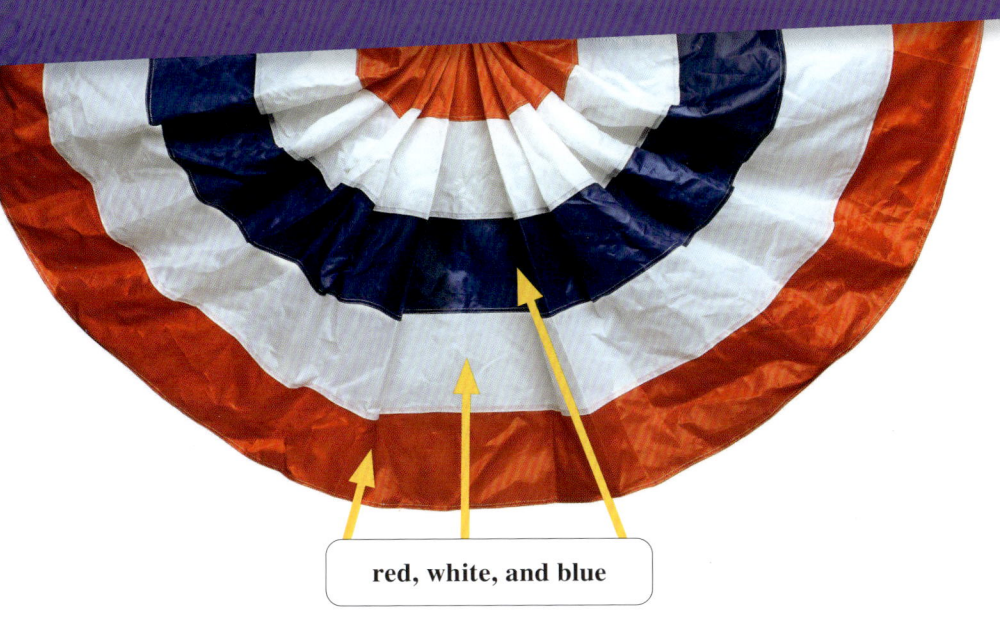

red, white, and blue

first flag
(1777)

Government Monuments

Washington Monument

Lincoln Memorial

Martin Luther King Jr.
Memorial

Jefferson
Memorial

Independence
Hall

Historical Founders

George
Washington

Thomas
Jefferson

Alexander
Hamilton

John
Adams

Samuel
Adams

Patrick
Henry

James
Madison

John
Marshall

George
Mason

Federal Government Holidays

New Year's Day
January 1

Martin Luther King Jr.'s Birthday
third Monday in January

Washington's Birthday
third Monday in February

Memorial Day
last Monday in May

Juneteenth National Independence Day
June 19

Independence Day
July 4

Labor Day
first Monday in September

Columbus Day
second Monday in October

Veterans Day
November 11

Thanksgiving Day
fourth Thursday in November

Christmas Day
December 25

Consultant
Cheryl Lane, M.Ed.
Secondary Teacher

Publishing Credits

Rachelle Cracchiolo, M.S.Ed., *Publisher*
Emily R. Smith, M.A.Ed., *SVP of Content Development*
Véronique Bos, *VP of Creative*
Fabiola Sepulveda, *Art Director*

Photo Credits: p.6 (bottom) Supreme Court of the United States; p.7 (top) Getty Images/
Mondadori Portfolio; p.7 (middle) Getty Images/Mark Wilson; p.8 (top) Getty Images/
Bloomberg; p.8 (middle) Alamy/UPI; p.9 (top) Alamy/Jim West; p.9 (middle) Getty Images/
Houston Chronicle/Hearst Newspapers; p.14 (top) Getty Images/MediaNews Group/Orange
County Register; p.16 (bottom) Alamy/Allstar Picture Library Ltd; p.17 (top) Getty Images/
Win McNamee; p.17 (bottom) Alamy/Marmaduke St. John; p.19 (bottom) Alamy/ Jeffrey Isaac
Greenberg 13+; p.20 (top) LOC[LC-DIG-ppmsca-59400]; p.20 (bottom) LOC[2021667570];
p.21 (top) National Archives; p.28 (bottom right) The White House Historical Association;
p.28 (bottom left) The White House Historical Association; p.29 (top) LOC[LC-USZ62-16369];
p.29 (top right) Alamy/Science History Images; p.29 (middle) The White House Historical
Association; p.29 (middle right) Library of Virginia; p.29 (bottom) Alamy/The Picture Art
Collection; all other images from iStock, Shutterstock, or in the public domain

Library of Congress Control Number available upon request.

5482 Argosy Avenue
Huntington Beach, CA 92649
www.tcmpub.com
ISBN 979-8-3309-0488-4
© 2025 Teacher Created Materials, Inc.
Printed by: 51497
Printed in: China